Writer's Block

A Collection of Poems For Black Women and Other Folks

AYANNA MONIQUE POOLE

Writer's Block

Copyright © 2020 Ayanna Poole

All rights reserved.

DEDICATION

To the black folks suffering from oppression and depression, systematically made to think they're crabs in a bucket but preparing to snap back. To the liberators, the educators, the nurturers and the nurtured. To my beautiful family, both by blood and joint tears for freedom. To the women that know of their magic but still search for purpose. To those affected by violence and hatred, but still find time to love. Asé.

This book was written in loving memory of my beloved great-grandparents and fellow revolutionaries, Rev. Marion Holland Wheeler, Sr. and Nora Jesmer Wheeler. Thank you for teaching me the power of the tongue and the significance of living in your truths. Without your guidance and wisdom, I can't imagine that this book would've ever come to fruition.

Journaling

what do you do
with open lines on pages
fixated idly between thoughts
in your journal,
what do you do
with those gaps,
between what you are
and what you are destined to be.

don't allow this to be
another journal with blank pages.

here

between the seals of these pages
you will find yourself
through the words never written
screaming for liberation.

here

you will see a child gasping for air
as you pull her from the city pool.
this is where
nobody else will have to save you.

    you are in control

Writers Never Stop Existing

this is the writer's block
where writers stop writing
but keep remembering
and savoring memories
that are tasteless
but full of flavor
enough seasoning to
gyrate on the tongue
until they are in the mouths
of others
and being reminded that
pens and papers
never stopped existing
and neither did I

,

Blood

this is how it feels to be a woman:
to wake with the sun to prepare your hair
and bodies to mirror the likes of lady-hood.

                              this is how it feels to be a black woman:
                                        to apply oil to our fingertips
                                        to untwist aloe vera tresses,
                                  to lift our roots with the picks
                                            of cotton's sons,
                                    to watch our hair transcend
                                      and rap megan lyrics
                                  until it is time to switch codes
                          from curls for the girls to corporate coils
                                            and be told
                              neither are acceptable hairstyles

this is how it feels to be a woman:
to endure pains once a month
with fire in your eyes inspired
by shades of your newest visitor.

                              this is how it feels to be a black woman:
                                      to feel fires in the belly
                                      every threesixtyfive
                                    that monthly cramps
                                  could never compare to

                                            to fear

                              the mahogany shaded body
                                    standing next to you
                                        or even yours
                                      could be taken
                                        in a moment

                                          to question

1

if monthly pains
are even worth it
because the governmental system
fails our reproduction system
before
we are even able to reproduce

sure we'd love to have chocolate babies
and bless them with hershey kisses
but we want them to be
dipped in gold
before they're dipped in statistics

sure white sista,
power to my pussy
but my people are still drowning
in their own blood

this is how it feels to be a woman:
to be boxed and labeled
silent and sassy

this is how it feels to be a black woman:
to be silenced
labeled sassy and sensitive
for speaking
"radical" thoughts

as if you have any choice but

to be conscious
to be black and woman
but they won't teach you
of your magic

to be alluded as
the bottom of the barrel
and spend your whole life explaining

that you are not a crab,
but you will snap back

to see feminism preached
by white women

and knowing that their liberation
is not yours

i hope that our strength
and perseverance
frightens you.

this is how it feels to be a woman:
a black woman:
this is how it feels
to know your magic
and fear your magic
all at the same damn time:
this is how it feels to be a woman.

Alkebu-Lan

from her mother's womb
she became conscious,
for every trickling water
that fed her soul,
she sprang
roots
a foundation for perseverance,
no matter what forces
attempted trauma to her stature,
it was here,
bellowing from her mother's belly
where she found herself

the queen of the sunflowers
dwelling where wells had gone dry,
she was
the one that blossomed
with little hydration

reigned

she was mystic,
became the bearer of gardens
placing seeds into her wounds
awakening life
the flowers, the trees and the writer alike
bowed to her seasons
danced with the sounds of her winds
worshipped the aroma of her sweetness,
honeycombs, marula oil and naartjies
she smelled like
a kemetic mother

from her womb
all things become conscious,
for every trickling water
that fed their soul,
they sprang
roots
the flowers, the trees and the writer alike

i didn't mean to offend you
but sometimes my heart
doesn't consult with my mind
before escapading off of my tongue
like callow cliff divers
failing to consider their landings
and today, you were the spit
my mouth cursed

if it's worth anything,
i am forever **apologetic**
for saying exactly what i feel

**god
bless the man
that blesses me
with literature**

that inserts
words
into my
fragmented
sentences

to help me write
this book

Schurz Hall

as we lie in bed, our union becomes lost
into the savagery of dark corners.
hunting such game should require license.
though lost souls may lose value—found will rise in cost.
but here we are in the depths of despair,
posing still that collapsing tightropes can bear
the weight of us both. we fall deeper than
the trenches of fire beneath us. this
is not love. this has never—

you know i love you, girl. right?

yeah, i love you too.

Art For Art's Sake

Amen-Ra, Zulu
humble I kowtow at your feet
asking you to rehabilitate our troops—
for some time during the war they were
offered portraits of white men
in exchange for their surrender and warfare
against our people

spineless they've become,
backs hunched, knees plunged into pavements,
two shackles—
attaching them to their comrades
as they vilely crawl past war protestors
and warriors bellowing,

"i thought you were a soldier, boy."
this is not a job for the weak.
this has never been a job for the weak.

Amen-Ra, Zulu
humble I kowtow at your feet
asking you to rehabilitate our troops—
for some time during the war
their pointers became demagnetized,
and they lost their direction.

Here, Forever

my grandfather was a mighty man,
waiting with a heavy heart on his world to change,
rocking in the late evening,
suspended from all previous understanding

i am told that hymns of his life flow through my poetry,
pouncing off the tongue to build fortresses in every space i speak.
they say my old shadowed soul holds stories of believers,
my eyes storerooms of waiting visions
that faultless pupils can't detect.

usually,
i repel the judgement
from fear
of narrow roads
and standing in boxes,
fear
that i can't quite feed these earthless fires,
fear
that no matter how mighty i may be polished,
i am crawling with mossed frameworks,
scattered by bloodless relations
layered with stained insecurities,
fear that i'd never *live* long enough
to emerge
from these cold corners
and here
forever
i'd be lined in journals

i wrote a poem for you,
so you'll live forever,
even if don't

Father's Day

i was raped
sunday morning
a couple miles away from the pulpit
as a young boy thanked
the only father he'd ever known
for protection

maybe if i made plans
to visit my father
who never wanted me
in his home
i wouldn't have been in yours

these four walls knew no filter
for every story it had ever been told
were pierced into its structure
blanketed with sweet hues of purple
its window's onlookers blind
to the notebook by the nightstand—blank
for no words had to be spoken
for what this room could tell
from remembrance
as if the play
were rehearsed a thousand times—
unconscious

5:55 AM

people are heading to work
the dogs are hungry
birds are singing songs of sovereignty
and i assume cock-a-doodle-doo
doesn't always mean good morning,
sometimes it means wake the fuck up

Trope

arms and legs flailed,
wide as the Potomac,
signaling the squirming,
the clenched fist,
the anger,
the self-distancing

at 4, temper tantrums
weren't signs of trauma,
they were signs of devil kids
who needed to gather their
4 inches of hands to collect
the limbs of the gum bumelia
for discipline

by 10, i was diagnosed
by family with
ADHD
Bipolar Disorder
ADD
Tourette's
ODD

and never,
could i get the chance
to communicate the disorder
of the mind marked by—
absent fathers
sexually abused cousins
school bullies
unpaid bills
uncultured teachers
switches and belts
curious minds
lingering and wondering
if speaking

was enough to give
me something to cry about
sexual attractions
white girl hair
versus bows and barrettes
sundays
the yelling
the screaming
the kicking

the only way i ever knew
how to express
anything

Reality T.V.

i'm not your television friend
when i find that the people around me
can be colder than christmas
i don't leave them
i invite them over
to sit under shade trees
and share some scorching-hot tea

Cologne Section

she inhales the cologne
of a man she's never met
as her head relaxes
on his shoulder
tongue licking lobes
one hand playing
in his locs
the other stretched
to his core
reaching
for something
she'd never known to be hers

"i'll take two"
for him
                         no,
for memory

Sunday Dreaming

when we sleep,
do you wonder what
we're dreaming
or do you ignore us,
count us dead
as lead-laced water
reaches up to our temples,
tight-ropes noosed
around our imagination
as we imagine a world
in which we can live
and learn and
not have to worry
that when we're dreaming,
law enforcement will bulge
into our place of refuge
and count us dead

count our dead

when we sleep
we are dreaming of a world
in which you don't exist,
but sometimes,
when we don't have control,
we dream of you,
and pray that we can wake up
fast enough to stay alive

-Aiyana Mo'Nay Stanley Jones

Labeled Fragile

she was paper thin
thin enough for you
to write your stories
and they'd bleed to
the other pages
of her book

cover anything
she had ever written
and claim this now
as her own

a storm
could blow her
away
rain piercing
into her cheeks
cracking
every word
lying beneath

Peace Nook

the smell of incense
and spiritual oils
linger between us

your head sinks
into my shoulder
as words of
wonderful women
roll off my tongue
like revolutions

our burdens
become lost
in unspoken words
resting between stanzas

eyes gazed
on the paper
we leave our worries
between covers

trust me..
they're better off
there

To Holland Jesmer, My Unborn

if i had the power to change seasons
i'd make spring last forever
because summers are too short
and i'd never want your autumn leaves to fall
and branches to go barren
when hearts grow cold

see i want spring to last forever
where youthfulness flows through hearts
and tears only fall to nurture the ground
you walk on
i want you to watch flowers blossom
and never question if they'll last
forever

Pillow Talk

head relaxed on your chest,
i find serenity in braille letters
as my fingers trace your sculpture.
even when our tongues don't
know the words, our souls speak
poetry in the silence.

i wonder
if what's never said
is more comforting
than what is.

                   leaping into white oceans
                tainted by bloody waters
             hoping that you are capable
          of swimming
        or completely drowning
     either is better than hallow corpses
hovering over an abyss of my tears

worse is falling

BELLS

ring.
the elation, the elevation
after my knees trembled
causing my feet to lose their placement
stumbling over for you
as fireworks filled my essence.
my body unbalanced on the pavement
lost
    confused
        fortunate
that you didn't leave like other prospects
in the past
what i'm really trying to say is:
yes!

i'm happy that you called.

Pando Gaze

wasps.
nests.
rocking chairs.
dirt daubers.
trees
that grow flowers.
cows.
horses
that i named
and don't remember.
quick sand.
cool breezes.
screen doors.
family reunions.
and you
reminding me:
all that is good
in the world
will last
forever.

New Ports

everything i touch
burns to ashes
sits in fire until
it's obsolete
even when i want it
to be absolute

i wonder if i want
to be loved more than
i ever wanted to love you
and selfishness is
the reason
i'm sitting in
infernos to light
cigarettes for sanity

Michael O.D. Brown Jr.

i remember
as if it were yesterday
laying in my full-sized bed
covers more disoriented
than my thoughts
and the only question
  the only question i never asked was why
i knew you hated us
from corners of corner stores
that sold Arizona teas and swishers
daps dedicated to liberation for me
and my niggas
the revolution will not be televised
it'll be on twitter
timelines flooded with images
and Canfield Green ~~tales~~ tells from the Lou
souls of folks screaming for freedom
that look just like you

and for the first time,
for the first time ever..
i was not afraid to prepare myself for war

Baggage

this is the portal you wanted
the one you prayed for
the one you wanted to wash away
your insecurities
until you were whole
after falling
breaking every meter
until you were no longer poetry
and here i go again
expecting this to be a poem about you
as if poetry makes me reach into a dimension
where i do not exist
and men are not used to leaving
or stay way longer than i want them to
even when i can't remember their names
and remnants of them rest on your shoulders
as remembrance of them makes me run
every time i get closer

i'm afraid to love you as i did in spring

frosting
doesn't make everything better
it makes it sweeter
easier to deal with
easier to go down
without forming lumps
in your throat
easier to rest on the tongue
and settle in the belly

Intentional

it is particularly sunny today
after the rain has kissed my skin
for seasons
for reasons we may never discuss

the rocks are stable
the water is running
the trees are waving
goodbye or hello

a young girl sits on
the bridge
questioning reality

then leaps
      on faith
            on fear

and realizes
that even the Virtues
can't save her

Redemption

i imagine that the road
to heaven is lined by trees
and the sun never sets
as the winds whisper affirmations
into your blood and
the streams wash your feet
of the sins that come
from running

when you said you needed **space**
i gave you an open yard,
let you run around frolicking
with the flowers,
let the weeds grow,
let you hoe it down,
'cause by then
i had lost patience

breathe.
i know right now
it feels like
the weight of the world
is on your shoulders,
it's only because you are still trying
to handle your own strength

breathe.
i promise everything will be okay

our pencils dance to the sounds of birds' stories
precious, yet flying or running from winter's past
we take advantage of the warmth between pages
to bury ourselves like cats in dark spaces
speaking only through people we have created
with wisdom of people we may never know
these books become houses passed by the wise
to marvel in the artificial **world of nothing**

the sharp sounds of confusion
continue to pull me here
listening to the **scents of**
Sauvage
telling me that love has not left
even if you have

maybe i am lonely and
living in memory
is much better
than living with nothing

scared that what you left
is much better than anything
i can ever find.

3AM Lovers

the direction of our records mimics
the music we play, songs telling stories
of circles and the baggage that continues
to pile into the carousel, moving fast as
money that never truly found its owner
but the pockets of you feels warm,
kissing at your thighs as we talk about
the weeping yellow jackets that bit off more
than they could chew...
this is how we sing
stinging and true
but only to last for the moment
even if it's a mistake

On 3AM Lovers

there is nothing more terrifying
than slowly decomposing into your sheets
after living in a fantasy of love
wasting into contradictions of childhood tales
that bid happy ever afters
these rooms become prisons
and as night falls
the mysteries screaming from the fireplace
remind us all that once had life
must say their goodbyes

and there is nothing
mortal hands can do
or sacrifice to whisper
life into the dead

Listening to *Man Down*

between every *i'm okay* are words
chambered in the pistol of the tongue,
stuck
 awaiting its release
waiting for you to make apologies
for unknown transgressions
before you're burned by bullets
of the tongue that only wanted you
to know its passions

things begin to take
the image of objects
or people
you once knew
when the time is right
and never for you
to know them again,

but for the lesson

Oak Cliff Nature Preserve

getting lost in you
is one of my passions
i can walk in circles
listening to hymns
of your belly, dancing
as the melody of your voice
shifts tempos or direction
because i know of all things
you are unchanging
and omnipotent
and only through you
will i ever find me

you are not God,
you are his voice
written in red
because no correction is needed.
you will never know corruption,
but too often destruction
as pale hands shake your foundation
for freedom
unknowing that you are the
greatest liberation

Never Enough

sometimes i speak too soon
want you to stay too long
run circles around my insecurities
until wrapped around you

sometimes i need too much
craving the love that my childhood
marked absent until you are no longer present

sometimes i cry too much
ignoring the fact that i am dying
from fear
until the only thing keeping me alive
is faith

but faith was never enough to make you stay

Cheryl's Mirror

fallen angels excavated her wounds
made home in her fears and distress
and now she sits across from you
giving comfort to depression
so that you may wake at the same time
as her tears
and find waters within yourself
running deeper than darkness hidden in
shadows

if the sun may shine again,
i hope that it finds you

Jonathan's Baby

i imagine you with a big ol' head
and skin so light yo daddy's folks question
if you yo daddy's baby at all.
i imagine you with a hair of wool,
playing loops of jazz as you
skid across the floor learning
to master the art
of movements.
i imagine your november-leafed eyes
and wide nose
stretched
 to understand
your surroundings.
i imagine you with tiny hands
outstretched for warmth
through your wintered tears.
i imagine your toes dancing
as little piggies go to the market.
i imagine your ears vibrating
with innocent sounds of the unheard
and opening your mouth to design
misinterpreted lyrics.

i imagine you full of life,
full of love,
full of fear,
full of us.

but most of all,
i imagine you a girl
bearing the same sentence
as our mothers' off springs
living in homes apart
or homes alone
or no home at all
and that's why most days,
i can't imagine you at all.

Covered in Concern

these covers know stories of rebellions
tears of terror
footsteps of faith
and the untitled,
the unsure,
but most of all
the unfrightened,
the ones who bear reverbs of sit-ins
and make their motions mimic movements
with 400 years of memories sprinting through their veins.

Let Me Touch Your Waves

collapse into my arms
and allow me dominance
over your oceans as you
rap to me lyrics
of prosperity. let me
weather your storms.
allow me to sail your
currents, peacefully
enduring the procession
of your waters
until i've found you
naked
without shackles
calm and floating
for freedom.

my first homicide
was at the age 11.
as the blood spewed
from her lips,
i clenched my chest
envisioning innocent things:

double dutch
hopscotch
barbies with maya
easy bake ovens
bunkbeds
slumber parties
vacation bible school
veggie tales.

from the porch,
the world looked less green
and more red.
i imagined this was
the making of a woman—
to know pain.
to replay the death
over and over.

i saw my first homicide
at age 11,
and every month,
i beg to be 10 again
and never know the pain
of losing everything
in the blink of an eye,
laying on madea's floor praying
that the world could be green again

and my panties could be white.

Square Business

old man butch always brought more
than candy and big texas to satisfy
his sweet tooth for chocolate babies
sitting on green-boxes in their texas daisies.
and most times, his snacks were free
if you were willing to pay.

that summer conversations no longer double dutched
or hula hooped but ran circles around the
old, white man preying on middle school girls
as their bosoms blossomed and hips expanded.

we could no longer dance on the porch
like we used to and snacks were no longer appealing
unless our mothers' food stamps were cut short
and we'd have to dance for you to
stop our stomachs from replaying the records
of poverty

...and for the first time ever,

i understood why mini vans came with precautions
and why you never trust white men
in black communities
but i said nothing.

i began playing house at the age of 5,
questioning if kissing could get me
pregnant
and imagining what a two mommy
household would look like.

my first kiss was a girl,
for hours
sleep-overs weren't half bad.
her lips tasted like ketchup,
that sweet sauce mommy never let me try
out of fear of making things messy,
so i did it anyway.
her tongue tasted like sunday mornings
with you.

we were just friends

Lunch Break

my cold heart yearns for warmth
until it's blanketed in forged fantasies
of affection carouseling your pretenses
through its veins to keep the cadences
of fairytales
at bay

July 4, 1993

i couldn't do any more sundays
eyes wandering in search of evening service gossip
with the ushers over pecan pie,
pastors humming you look good this mornings
so that he could spend church's offering
to make you his evening service,
old folks laying hands on the wedlocked
mother to pray forgiveness
forgetting they're no widow or no saint,
reminders to come as you are
but not make yourself seen
because calls to the alter
carry the fancy of new york runways
and parking lot pimps looking for more than prayer
holy trinities without vaginas as the alpha and omegas
no...

sundays are for making babies

Writer's Diet

i was consumed by unwritten parts of you
until they threatened pieces of me,
created garbled expressions of you
left stained like my fragmented lipstick
planted on your tongue
so that you may emulate
my definition of love

sojourned to restricted destinations
in this collage of my existence,
coddling my tears between your fingertips
until they could be used at my jeopardy

and now the thought of what we'd written
is indigestible,
falls like fire at the pit of my stomach
and you no longer have permission to guide
my pen to fashion your thoughts

sunday brunches
turn into sisterhood sit-ins
sharing life's newest renovations
over martinis and mimosas
converting from cordial to
organic conversations
as our tongues become deviant
against our baptist textiles and pantyhose
sharing words we'd stashed away
only for the weekends

on sundays,
we tattoo our sister's names
on our hearts
measure our wingspan
and get fly
share laughs induced by pain
and temporarily specialize in
sooth-saying to save one
another from becoming
another man's toy
he's hoarding in his garage

we drink until our bodies and faces
fashion friday nights
and worry is no longer welcome

Instinct

as the musical notes
abandon their lyrics
to kiss my lips,
i wonder if the beat
of this song travelled
the distance from
your heart
to find me,
tap-danced across
the horizon to align
with my moons,
filmed the sun rising
and kissed the land
with lavender,
so that
i may walk
calm and free,
whispered through leaves
w/ arbitrary instruments
that would play at my window
and lead me to you

as we question our existence in secret,
the pendulum continues to swing
over chutes of champagne
mocking the satchels we use
to carry our baggage until springtime,
burdened by the cold of the winter
our memory denies colors
in spaces that have become barren,
and we become sentiments of April skies
burying puddles into bedtime prayers
and bedtime accounts of anxiety.
we lack the transparency to see truth
through transitions and find ourselves
here..
watching **solar eclipses** in search of meaning.

Hopkins County Memorial Hospital

down the street from where my first pencil
touched paper to carve letters
into pages to let people know
i am here
you held my first breath
and my madea's last

down the street from
my first home
my first friend
my first kiss
my first freedom
my first memory
of the moon choosing me
to be its focal point

you held people captive
souls swaying through the air
as distant memories become
last breaths
and resurrections of new life

and everything around us
disintegrates until it no longer
has lips to tell, only ears to hear
the cries of the lady in room 126
that doesn't know if this is the beginning
or the end

Pacific Park

sundays are for passing love letters
down the pew to the boy
with the big nose
that momma said stay away from.
she never too much liked
the color yellow

i guess that's why we slept until
the sun set west and bid us adieu
or God be with you's
as she is every Sunday
when the waistband of my daisy dukes
hugs my skin
in ways that dresses never could.

sundays are for snowcones,
glaciers relinquishing themselves
to mimic our movements
fluid as our hips
as Donnell reminds the elderly
we know what's up
even in the summer of 1999.

sundays are for booty popping
when we are far enough from our
mommas that we can't
get our booties popped.

on the other side of the park,
we grew faster than we ever
could on the playground.

surrounded by slabs and gold chains
we learned that sundays..
                sundays are for lovers

East Caney

patiently reading in between narrations
of decade-stained aloe photos,
i find myself toothless,
buried in the newness of summertime afternoons
in 2000's East Caney.
when i was the sun's daughter,
bathed in collard greens and cornbread
i was 7. the closest to God i'd ever been.
sewed Genesis and Revelations together
so that the blood of the blackberries
could be buried into the soil to create mud
for the dirt daubers
that would never know my name
to be as sweet as peach cobbler,
but always remember home.

Free Yourself

as the blood drips from the book
evil loses its livelihood
becomes as reminiscent as
summer's pink skies in the dark of the winter
reminds the pages that hold tribute that without pain
there is no room for love and beauty
even diamonds cannot form without pressure
but truth and light has chosen you
to speak life
through the mysteries of love
no longer do you have to hold the honor
of the heartbroken

Shining Armor

i haven't been coping
in ways that i need to
i sacrificed myself
so i could free you

when i haven't even freed myself

no poetry in months.
for my pen,
there were no new strokes.
no new notes playing
from vinyls spinning.
i sacrificed sound

silenced by "i understands"
and "i'll do betters", whispering
as light as chicago winds
in deep-fried weathers.

i wonder if poetry
ever gets tired of saving me.

Confluence

battered and berried since
my breast knew how to rumba
into training bras
i learned how to use my fists
to write poetry
my words pummeled into your face
with nothing but an apology
dancing on my tongue
as my story seeps into gashes
frantically searching for asylum

i can recall the look upon your face
as if it were my own and somehow
i feel connected to you
like the ring around the rosies,
imagining ashes are the only thing
to stop the pounding
from simulating bruises
onto the conscience

law of energy states:
energy cannot be destroyed,
only transferred
and i wonder if you know
my pain
can feel it
buckling in your knees
before you collapse
and the ground becomes
a sentiment of oceans
i've cried many times before

I Teach 7th Grade

and i am the newest hallway gossip
underdeveloped and well-aged children
glare questionably at my belly
sometimes to rub, to peek,
to make inferences about
what is growing inside

some even ask

"Ms. P, you pregnant?"

i smile and tell them

"get to class
and mind your business."

i am reminded why i hated middle school
and why i loved it all at the same time
it was okay to be curious
to ask questions
to look at the world around me
and care more about others
than myself
but being the new talk
never comes with popularity
unless you were the teacher
growing in ways
that children will one day understand

i am not pregnant
the only thing bubbling down there
are reminders
that children
are mean
as hell.

but Honest.

Club Reo

i knew how to make
my hips roll at a young age.
i knew all of the tricks
and how to flip them,
could even work
a magician's stick
if i needed to.
i knew the caged bird
sang to nicki lyrics
before i ever
understood why maya
lives in metaphors.

walking in circles
became more common
as mixtures of alcohol
and caffeine streamed
into our blood
to collect samples
for Tyler's next cycle.
we wore the fragrance
of black 'n milds
and swishers,
and brought friday
mornings in with the
adults we'd become

if we were lucky.

as the sun makes motions
to stick our skin,
we open the house door
to feel a cool breeze
against aunt joann's
refusals to cool off
the entire neighborhood.
through the screen door,
we can smell fried chicken
cabbage
sweet potatoes
but outside
summertime
wreaks of
blue magic
and braid spray
splits roads through my hair
with nothing more than
a rat-tail comb
yanking coils loose
to make way
for rows of corn
weaving in and out
to make me "pretty,
you wanna be pretty
don't chu, yannie?"

painfully sitting
on the concrete porch
in between coco's frail legs
waiting to be popped in
the back of my head for
trying to see if she is
almost finished
and in secrecy
i ask God
to be **a boy,**
just **for the season.**

Skeletons

sometimes being a woman
means deciphering whether
my body is a temple or
a necropolis,
where the flesh comes
to mourn the skeletons of
its closet with newfangled words
to alleviate the affliction of
previous expressions
before the demise,
to be affirmed
that all that is dead
has not yet departed,
compelling my tombs to recite
their mantras as they retire
their tears and find solace
in souls that have not been
forgotten

in realizing that
god is woman,
i understand why
man could never
help me heal,
could never resurrect
abaddon from
hosting his spirits
in my wounds
and making them
a place of destruction,
and why in trusting him,
i always lost **sight**
of myself

when women are raped,
they learn how to love
                pain.
they learn how to surrender
and sacrifice nothing but
themselves,
holding dreams captive
in the beds of kingdoms,
underneath fools,
where no gold will ever be
rewarded
for bravery
for survival
for learning that
-
the art of loving can
only be attained when
one sacrifices
the burdened treasure
buried within themselves
until they are without

C Hall

seventh grade girls
will bicker and fight
over boys who can't
read or write
in their native tongue
and teach you that
history always repeats
itself and someone,
anyone, should've cared
about them both

it's never bright
to kill your prey
where they sleep,
     they will **haunt** you
         seek you through visions
and their predecessors
will rise
and conquer
and fall
and be victorious,
for they were never
dead at all

i fall in love before enjoying the moment,
make blueprints for homes and children
before knowing suns
and moons and risings
and idiosyncrasies
and sometimes names,
touch tongues and bodies
directly after touching my last
cup of Hennessy

thank God for best friends
and their **reminders**
to get our heads out of our asses.

The Interview

before you schedule me
into your business plans
be sure that you are ready
to make such investments,
the job is time-consuming
but you'll get paid by the hour,
by the minute, by the seconds
that you are connected to me
for the food i prepare is for the
body, for the soul,
for the long nights you
prayed for more

but such partners do not come by cheap
you will have to sacrifice

Sketchbook

make poetry graphic
let your black letters
dangle from trees
make the leaves burn
write in red
write bullet ballads
ink bleeding
black blood
on white paper
have your fingers
make similes like stones
make my poetry black

The Cookout

i like my barbecues black
dominoes slamming against
folding tables as unc yells
"get yo bitch ass up"
this is not a place for the weak

children reminding us how easy
it is to make friends, have fun and
still get in trouble for minding your
damn business because "didn't i tell y'all
asses to quit running in and out this house"

aunties gossiping about you or to you
because hennything is possible
unless they went down to the corner
to buy their favorite cheap spirits
and gossip becomes family secrets
of arguments to be recited in detail
at the next family cookout

nobody can be illiterate,
you must stay ready to read

this is not a place for the weak

For You

i'm always talkin' in third person
attempting to extract myself
from the pores of my poetry
so that you may hide
in between iambics,
go behind bolded letters
to scream
but never
seek me.
these poems are for you.

Cleanse

yesterday, i wore red.
permitted my hips to collide
with whispering trees
in search of the drummer,
connected with the earth
through my toes,
became the roots,
became the lifeline,
became the soil,
became the soul.

my skin speaks in truth
and light and love
and everything above

you see the sun loves me
came down from the heavens
just to place its lips on my surface
burying itself deep enough
into my body that when i am shot
blood splattered across the concrete
resembles painting of ancestral grounds
and revolutions
call this temple art

i am a walking negro spiritual
my tongue mimics mantras of rebellion
hurdling from cargo ships
because i choose freedom over captivity
use these lungs to rebuke shackles
and shout power into my people
set aside burden and wash my feet
to jump into the Jordan
where all prayers are promised
and the sun within me is allowed its place
to commence as the only rightful owner
of life
these limbs are the roots of your foundation
for without me, you are nothing
and with me, you are everything

i am the **Garden of Eden**

here
you can find me
often forgotten, sometimes
forbidden
to exist
but always becoming
the fruit of your labor

i wonder if you'll even care
to guard your captive crops
that have not been seen or heard

for **we,**
the black children of the ghetto
are the food of your foundation
without us, you will starve
we are the children of the sun
we are melanin in its purest form
we are black
and no energy can escape
we are absorbing, allow us to be
what our ancestors always wanted
we are the seeds in the pipes
that stop your pipelines from working
we are not your statistics
we are your architects
and your engineers
we are your future
we set records and break them
we are the only culture you know
from the womb to the classrooms
we are unbreakable
sit these blues on your tongue
longer
we are the rhythm in your movement
we are writers and this is our interlude
we are creatives
if only you allow us to be

the black children of the ghetto
with the sun in our eyes and souls,
allow us to be
the crops that will keep you fed

Long Live

i may never bear the pain
of your mothers,
grappling to understand
that the absence of the physical
doesn't mean the soul has flown away

i may never bear the pain
of your brothers,
questioning fights from childhood
that bare no significance
but weigh heavy in the heart

i may never bear the pain
of you,
begging in the last minutes
for time machines and
second chances to
call
text
love
live

but i will always bear the pain
of a friend,
who saw the world in your eyes
and wanted nothing more than
to make sure
you live forever.

For Harvey Thompson, Donovan Reese, Michael Phillips, Caleb
Black, Cedric Caddell, Laprida Shears, Jarrett Mosby, Mack
Johnson, Twin McGee, K'Darius Johnson and...

———————————————————

Use this space to journal or doodle your feelings, reactions and experiences while reading this book. Post on Instagram, Twitter or Facebook using hashtag #WritersBlock2020.

Ayanna Poole

COVER ART CREDITS

Muse: Jhané Johnson
Instagram: @jhanerachel
Twitter: @thejhanerachel

Graphic Designer: Wilfred Will Uche
Twitter or Instagram: _artofwill

ABOUT THE AUTHOR

Ayanna Monique Poole is an American writer, teacher, and civil rights organizer from East Texas, best known for her contributions to the revitalization of the black student body movement through Concerned Student 1950. She received a BA in English Literature from the University of Missouri, with emphases in Creative Writing and African American Literature. She developed her love for literature and liberation at a young age as she begged for answers to her challenging questions about the world around her. In her first book, Writer's Block, she explores memoirs of her experiences as the continues to get a grasp of life. She currently resides in Grand Prairie, TX. You can find her on:

Twitter: jesmersdaughter
IG: yannamo_
Facebook: Ayanna Monique
Website: www.jesmerbooks.com

Made in the USA
Columbia, SC
04 June 2020